the magical science of feelings

train your amazing brain to:

quiet anger ⚡ soothe sadness 💧 calm worry 🧡 share joy

JEN DAILY, LICSW

Illustrations by Gwen Millward

Storey Publishing

Feelings can seem magical, can't they?

It's like they just appear out of nowhere . . . **POOF!**

Or maybe it's like you **drank a magic potion** that made your body feel different all of a sudden.

Like when you go from **super silly . . .**

to **out of control!**

Have you noticed feeling **low and slow** when you are sad?

Does your tummy feel funny when you are scared or nervous?

How does your body feel when you are **happy?**

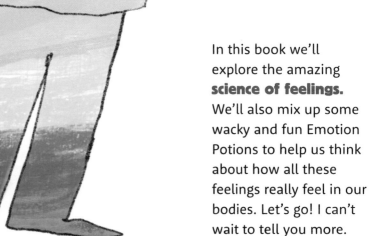

Poof!

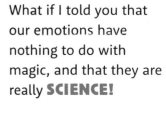

What if I told you that our emotions have nothing to do with magic, and that they are really **SCIENCE!**

If our feelings are science, not magic, that means we can learn where they come from and try to **understand what's happening in our bodies.** Neat!

In this book we'll explore the amazing **science of feelings.** We'll also mix up some wacky and fun Emotion Potions to help us think about how all these feelings really feel in our bodies. Let's go! I can't wait to tell you more.

Where do feelings come from?

The science of feelings starts with our brains. Did you know that humans have the most complicated brains of all the animals in the world? Our brains have many different parts, but I'd like to introduce you to the **four parts of our brains** that have to do with our feelings. Each one has an important job.

These four brain parts are our best friends when it comes to understanding our emotions. They also work together to make us . . . us!

Meet Amy!

AMYGDALA

Amy's job is to listen to all of our senses and make sure we're safe. If she *thinks* we're not safe, she sends out the alarm!

Meet Hippo!

HIPPOCAMPUS

Hippo's job is to learn and remember. Hippo even recognizes patterns so we can move smoothly through our days.

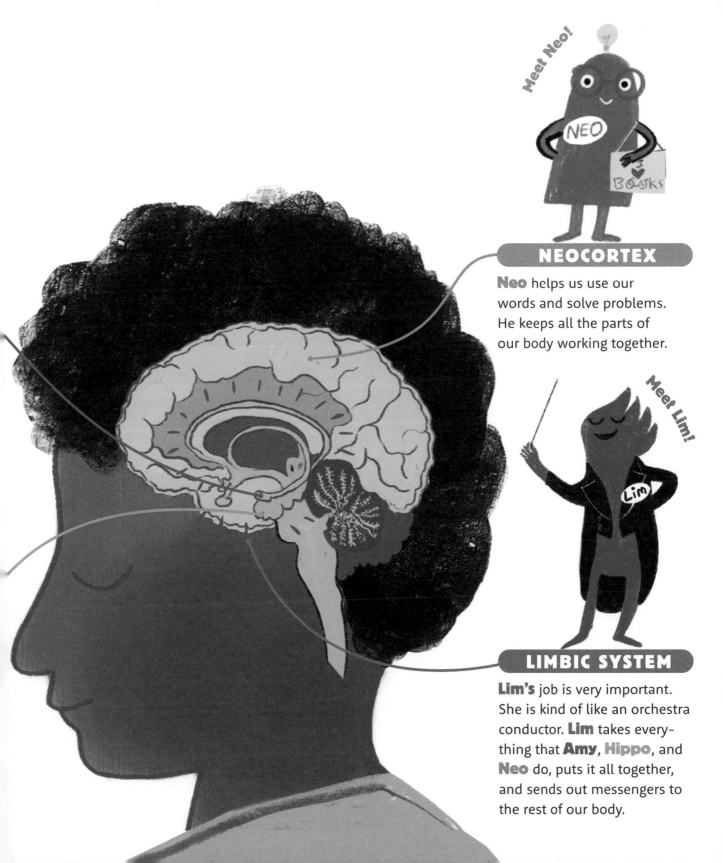

Meet Neo!

NEOCORTEX

Neo helps us use our words and solve problems. He keeps all the parts of our body working together.

Meet Lim!

LIMBIC SYSTEM

Lim's job is very important. She is kind of like an orchestra conductor. **Lim** takes everything that **Amy**, **Hippo**, and **Neo** do, puts it all together, and sends out messengers to the rest of our body.

Meet the messengers

As our brain's conductor, **Lim** sends out different kinds of messengers.

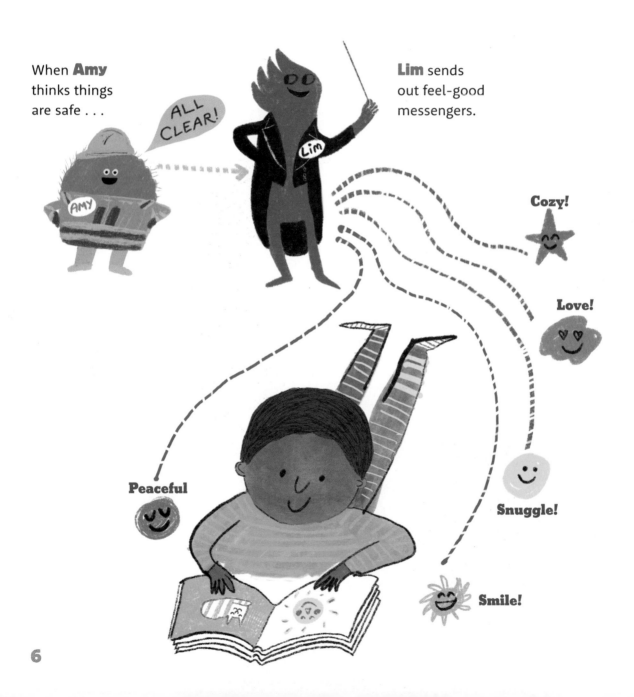

When **Amy** thinks things are safe . . .

ALL CLEAR!

AMY

Lim

Lim sends out feel-good messengers.

Cozy!

Love!

Peaceful

Snuggle!

Smile!

When **Amy** thinks there may be danger . . .

Lim sends out messengers to help us get out of danger.

Scream!

Fight!

Run away!

Hide!

Ack!

Teamwork

Lim's messengers have big names. They are called **neurotransmitters**, **hormones**, and **endorphins**.

There are at least 40 different neurotransmitters and other messengers in our bodies. That's a lot. And **Lim** makes sure all these messengers work together all day long, without us even noticing!

They have a lot to do with our feelings, as you'll see in the rest of this book.

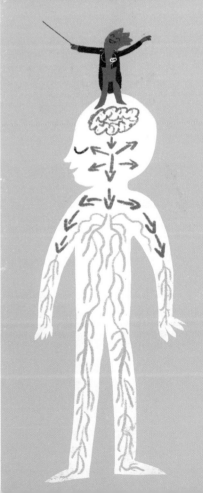

Calm down, Amy!

Have you ever noticed that when you are having A LOT of feelings about something, it's hard to think? That's **Amy** shouting over **Neo** and **Hippo**.

Lim tries to listen to everybody and send out the right messengers to keep you safe.

But sometimes **Amy** gets really worked up, and then **Amy** gets loud.

Sometimes **Amy** is SO LOUD, **Lim** can't hear what **Neo** and **Hippo** have to say.

DANGER!

The louder **Amy** shouts her danger signals, the faster **Lim** responds.

There are lots of things we can do to calm **Amy** down, and to help **Lim** listen to everyone.

Let's explore the ways we can calm down and balance our feelings.

happy

Chances are, you know exactly what it feels like to feel happy. Happiness puts a smile on our face, a giggle in our voice, and warm fuzzy feelings all over. When we are happy, it's like a warm sunbeam is following us everywhere.

What's happening in my body when I feel happy?

When we feel happy, **Lim** sends out many different messengers.
These messengers create happiness when they work together,
just like how instruments played together can create beautiful music.

Meet the Happiness Messengers

The four main messengers of happiness are dopamine, oxytocin, serotonin, and endorphins.

Dopamine is all about rewards. You know that good feeling you get after doing a hard thing, or hearing someone say something nice about you? That's dopamine, encouraging you to do that thing again.

Oxytocin is the messenger of love! While dopamine gives a quick reward, oxytocin lasts a long time. **Lim** often sends out oxytocin when we snuggle, helping us feel calm, safe, and loved.

Serotonin is one of **Lim's** most important messengers. The more serotonin **Lim** sends out, the happier we feel. Serotonin is made in our brains *and* our bellies. It helps us digest our food, feel good about ourselves, and feel like we are important.

Endorphin is a word for more than 20 different brain messengers. Endorphins are pretty amazing. They help us feel less pain, help us feel good about ourselves, and make things we enjoy feel even better.

What makes you happy?

Our brains are so cool. Did you know that we can help **Lim** send out happiness messengers just by thinking about things that make us happy? What are some things that make you feel happy?

Playdate with my best friend

Grandma coming to visit

Puppy kisses

Birthday presents

A thank-you note to Lim

Let's take a moment and say thank you to **Lim** for all the ways she helps us feel! You can use the words in this example to get you started. If you need help, ask a grown-up to write for you. You can also draw a picture.

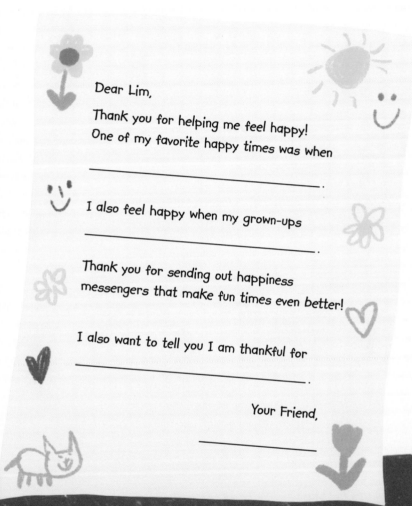

Dear Lim,

Thank you for helping me feel happy! One of my favorite happy times was when

_____.

I also feel happy when my grown-ups

_____.

Thank you for sending out happiness messengers that make fun times even better!

I also want to tell you I am thankful for

_____.

Your Friend,

_____

How Does Being Thankful Make Us Happier?

Did you know that sharing our thankfulness with others actually makes us happier? It's one of the ways our bodies make more serotonin. I'm so thankful for the scientists who have studied our brains and shared their knowledge with all of us!

Make an EMOTION POTION!

SILLY SLIME

We can help **Lim** send out more happiness messengers when we do silly and fun things! Playing with slime can be pretty silly, and it's always a lot of fun.

YOU'LL NEED

- 8 ounces white school glue
  - A plastic bowl and a rubber spatula
  - A few drops of food coloring
- 1 tablespoon baking soda
  - Contact lens solution
  - Googly eyes

1 Mix the glue and food coloring in a bowl. Start with one or two drops of food coloring, adding more to get the color you want.

2 Mix in the baking soda.

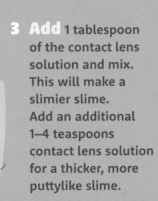

3 Add 1 tablespoon of the contact lens solution and mix. This will make a slimier slime. Add an additional 1–4 teaspoons contact lens solution for a thicker, more puttylike slime.

PLAY WITH YOUR SLIME!

Can you squish it to make silly sounds?
What happens when you hold it with your fingers spread open?

To make your slime even sillier, try mixing in some googly eyes!

Does your slime make you **GIGGLE?** **Lim** sends out lots of feel-good endorphins when we **LAUGH.** Laughter also helps us relax our body.

Do you feel **HAPPY** when you play with your slime?

How does **HAPPINESS** feel in your body?

Make a family joy jar

Like most feelings, happiness has a lot of different names. Sometimes we might use the words *joy* or *joyful*, or we might use the word *silly*, which is also a kind of happiness.

Scientists have learned that sharing our joy with others makes us feel happier than if we just kept that joy all to ourselves. Make a family Joy Jar to see how it works!

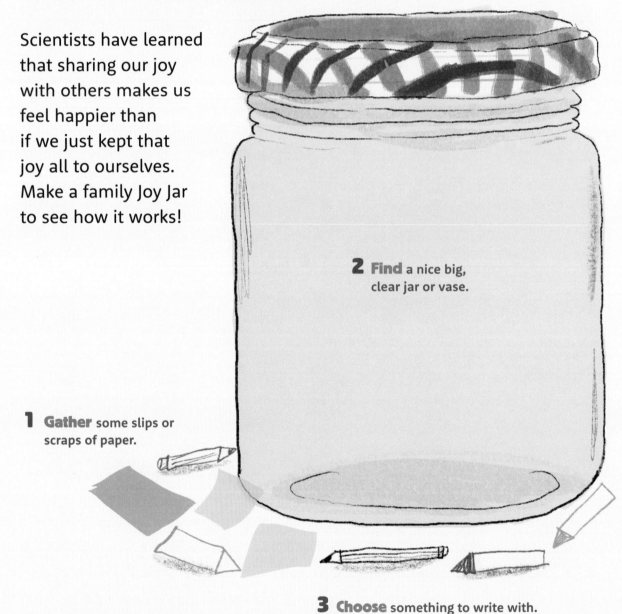

2 Find a nice big, clear jar or vase.

1 Gather some slips or scraps of paper.

3 Choose something to write with.

4 **Each evening,** sit down with your family, and write or draw a joyful moment from your day.

5 **Place** those moments of joy in the Joy Jar.

Everyone in the family can write down their joyful moments.
If you have a family pet, or a baby in the family, you could even guess what might have been a joyful moment for them!

Once a week, take out the slips of paper and share them with one another. Notice how much more joy you feel when you share your joy with others!

19

sad

Have you ever seen a cartoon where a little rain cloud follows someone who is sad? A magical cloud sprinkling you with raindrops of sadness isn't really how sadness works, is it?

When we are sad, sometimes it feels like our heart aches. We might cry. Sadness can make us feel low and slow, but it can also make us feel out of control.

What's happening in my body when I feel sad?

Our brain friends **Amy** and **Hippo** have a lot to do with feeling sad.

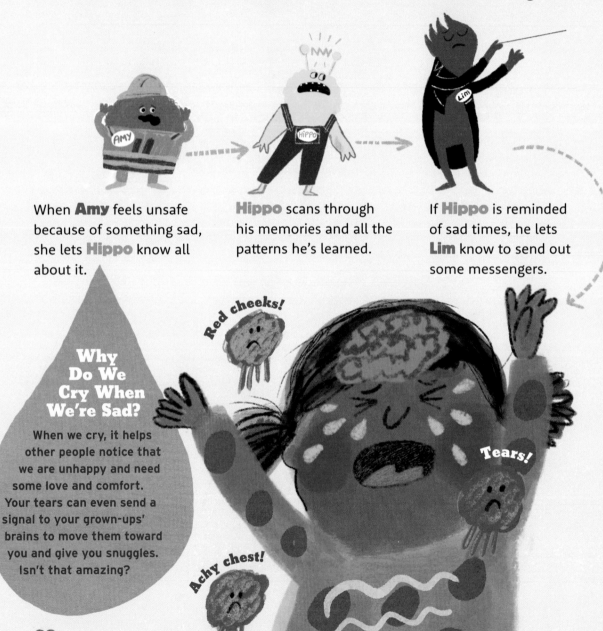

When **Amy** feels unsafe because of something sad, she lets **Hippo** know all about it.

Hippo scans through his memories and all the patterns he's learned.

If **Hippo** is reminded of sad times, he lets **Lim** know to send out some messengers.

Red cheeks!

Tears!

Achy chest!

Why Do We Cry When We're Sad?

When we cry, it helps other people notice that we are unhappy and need some love and comfort. Your tears can even send a signal to your grown-ups' brains to move them toward you and give you snuggles. Isn't that amazing?

Inside your grown-up's brain, **Lim** is also sending messengers, telling them you might need a hug!

Have you ever noticed that when you feel sad, your body moves toward someone you love and trust? That's **Lim** sending a messenger to tell our muscles to go find someone safe.

oxytocin

The Magic of Hugs

Once you feel safe and protected in your grown-up's arms, **Lim** sends out some cozy, loving oxytocin messengers.

What makes you sad?

While we all feel sadness, we don't all feel it for the same reasons.

?

I made
a bad
mistake.

I lost
my soccer
game.

My brother
broke
my bike.

?

My
cat ran
away.

My
friend
was mean.

I hurt
my knee.

I feel
lonely.

Grandma
is sick.

Did thinking about this sad stuff make you feel a little sadder?

That's **Amy** and **Hippo** working together, noticing your memories and patterns.

I wonder, did you just snuggle in with a friend or grown-up when you felt a bit sad?

That's **Lim** telling you to go find someone to make you feel better.

Do you feel less sad now?

It's your amazing brain at work!

Make an
EMOTION POTION!

SADNESS GOO

This potion moves slowly sometimes, feels hard when you try to catch it, and will definitely cheer you up when you play with it!

YOU'LL NEED

A few drops of food coloring

2 cups cornstarch

1 cup water

Mix all the ingredients in a medium-size bowl until you have a smooth, wet goop!

PLAY WITH YOUR SADNESS GOO!

Notice how the Sadness Goo moves and changes.
How does sadness feel like this in your body?

What happens
when you let the goo
run **SLOWLY** between
your fingers?

When has
sadness felt
HARD OR FAST?

When has
sadness felt
LOW AND SLOW
in your body?

What happens
when you
squeeze it or try
to catch it fast?

Getting un-sad

We all feel sad now and then. It's just part of being human. But sadness doesn't last forever, I promise! Sadness always goes away, sometimes sooner, sometimes later.

When we just don't want to feel sad anymore, we need a plan to help us get un-sad. There are things we can do to change what messages our brains send and receive.

Play

Talk to a loved one

What else helps you get un-sad?

Going outside to swing?
Spending time with a pet?
Making art?

Instead of thinking,
try using **your senses**!
Snuggle a pet or stuffed
animal. **Smell** a flower.
Listen to the birds
or your favorite song.

Doing these things
helps **Lim** send out
new messengers that
make us feel better.

Cotton-ball breathing

Have you ever felt out of control with your sadness?
Maybe you couldn't stop crying, or were even having a hard time catching your breath!

When lots of emotion is happening all at once, that's called **being overwhelmed** (see page 55). This happens when our friend **Lim** sends too many messengers all at once.

But guess what? We can send a new signal that tells **Lim** "enough!"

YOU'LL NEED:

A cotton ball
A straw

1 Place the cotton ball on a table in front of you.

2 Put the straw in your mouth. Take a BIG breath in while counting to 4.

3 Now blow the cotton ball across the table while you count to 8.

Keep practicing! Can you get the cotton ball to move steadily across the table?

4 **Once** you feel like you are in control of your breath, stop using the cotton ball and just breathe through the straw.

5 **Breathe in** for a count of 4.

Breathe out for a count of 8.

Do this 4 times.

Finally, take one more REALLY big breath in, and then release.

How do you feel?

Congratulations! You've just learned to tell **Lim** to stop sending overwhelming messages! You can use this breathing skill whenever you feel overwhelmed with any emotion.

mad

Have you ever seen a character in a cartoon
get mad? How did you know they were mad?
Did you see steam shooting out of their ears?
Or flames coming from the top of their head?
Or maybe their face was scrunched up tight
and their cheeks got red. That's MAD, all right!

What's happening in my body when I feel mad?

When we feel mad, it's because **Amy** has noticed something doesn't feel quite right.

Lim sends out messengers so we can be ready to fight to make it right, if we have to.

Those messengers make us scrunch up our face and ball our fists, and maybe our cheeks get red. This sends a message to other people to stay back!

Red face

Shouting

Tight fists

Stomping

Why Do I Want to Hit and Stomp?

When we feel mad, **Lim** sends messengers lickety-split! Those messengers, called **adrenaline** and **cortisol**, rush into the big muscles in our arms and legs, giving them extra energy. That's why when we feel mad, we want to hit and stomp!

Have you ever done something when you were mad that you felt sorry about later?

I feel bad for saying mean things to my mommy. I wish I knew how to make it better . . .

NEO

That's **Neo** catching up and helping us think through what went wrong.

When you're ready, it is important to say you are sorry, and ask how to make it better. This is a good time for you and your grown-ups to practice coping skills like the ones you're about to learn on pages 40 and 42. Then you can use those skills the next time you are mad.

A COPING SKILL is a way to take care of our feelings before they get out of control.

What makes you mad?

Everyone feels mad sometimes, and people get mad for all sorts of different reasons. When people are hungry or tired, they might be more likely to feel mad. Have you ever noticed that?

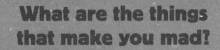

I want that ball!

She cut me in line!

?

It's not fair!

I don't want to go to bed!

?

Different words for mad

Did you know that *mad* and *angry* are the same feeling?
What are some other words you know that mean mad or angry?

Do different words feel like different ways of being mad?

What does your body feel like when you are **furious?**

How about when you're **frustrated?**

What does your body feel like when you're **annoyed?**

ANGER VOLCANO

Mad is a tricky feeling because it is the fastest-moving feeling there is! Sometimes it feels like a volcano erupting in our chest. This potion helps us to see just how quickly we can go from feeling in control to feeling out of control when we feel mad.

Make an EMOTION POTION!

YOU'LL NEED

- 4 tablespoons baking soda
- A small jar or cup
- A liquid measuring cup
- 1 cup vinegar
- A few drops of food coloring (optional)
- An eyedropper or baster

TIP!
Do this activity in the sink or tub. It can get a little messy and out of control!

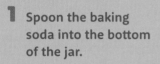

1 Spoon the baking soda into the bottom of the jar.

2 In the liquid measuring cup, mix the vinegar with the food coloring.

3 Using the eyedropper or baster, slowly add a few drops of vinegar to the jar of baking soda. Talk about what is happening!

4 When you are ready, pour all the vinegar into the jar of baking soda, and watch your **MAD VOLCANO** erupt!

LOOK AT ALL THAT FIZZ!

What happens as you start to add drops of vinegar to the baking soda?
What happens when you pour in all the vinegar?

Does anger sometimes feel like it is **BUBBLING AND FIZZING** deep in your body?

Can you think of a time when it felt like a big volcano **ERUPTING**? If so, what happened?

Stomp away the anger storm

Have you ever heard the saying that laughter is the best medicine? Well, when it comes to feeling mad, it's true! It's very difficult to go from mad to calm, but much easier to go from mad to silly, and then silly to calm.

Try this! Pick out a favorite song, one that feels really good to jump around to. Pretend to be Very Mad (it can help to think of a time you really did feel mad). Now try stomping around to your song.

Dance and stomp as hard as you can! When you are done, notice if your muscles are feeling more relaxed.

Stomping feels so good when we are mad because it helps our **adrenaline** and **cortisol** messengers work their way out of our muscles.

Why am I getting giggly now?

Did you start giggling and smiling a little when you were stomping around in that silly way?

That's **Lim** sending out feel-good messengers called **endorphins.**

Scan and squeeze the mad away

Have you ever been so mad that grown-ups have told you to take a time-out or go to your room? Have you ever felt like that made you **EVEN MADDER**? Sometimes it's hard to know how to settle down. Here's something that might help.

1 First, lie down and close your eyes . . .

2 Imagine a bright light shining on your toes and feet. Squeeze them tight and then let them feel loose.

3 Next, imagine the light scanning up your legs. Squeeze your legs as tight as you can and then let them relax.

Why Do I Feel Calmer?

When we pay attention to our bodies and how they feel in the moment, we can help our muscles relax. Relaxing our muscles on purpose helps **Lim** know that we are safe, so she can stop sending messengers like adrenaline and cortisol.

5 **Finally, imagine the light scanning over your neck and face.** Scrunch your face up tight and relax it again.

4 **Now imagine that light moving to your belly,** chest, arms, and hands. Squeeze them tight and then let them relax.

Now imagine the light scanning back down your body. Notice if you feel mad or tense anywhere. Squeeze and release those parts as you scan back down to your toes.

Keep scanning, squeezing, and relaxing until you feel calmed down.

43

worried

Did you know that every human being on the planet feels worried sometimes? Worry can feel like a swirly tightness in our chests, or butterflies in our bellies. When we are very worried, it can even feel like it's hard to breathe!

We have many names for feelings of worry. *Scared* and *nervous* are worried feelings. What are some other names of feelings that are close to feeling worried?

What's happening in my body when I feel worried?

When **Amy** thinks that danger might be nearby, she quietly lets **Lim** know.

Lim, **Hippo**, and **Neo** whisper together to make a plan.

If **Hippo** and **Neo** agree
that danger might be nearby,
Lim sends out messengers
to get our body ready.

Our eyes get big
so we can see better,
and our hearts pump
harder to help move
energy to our muscles
so we can run or fight
or hide if we need to!

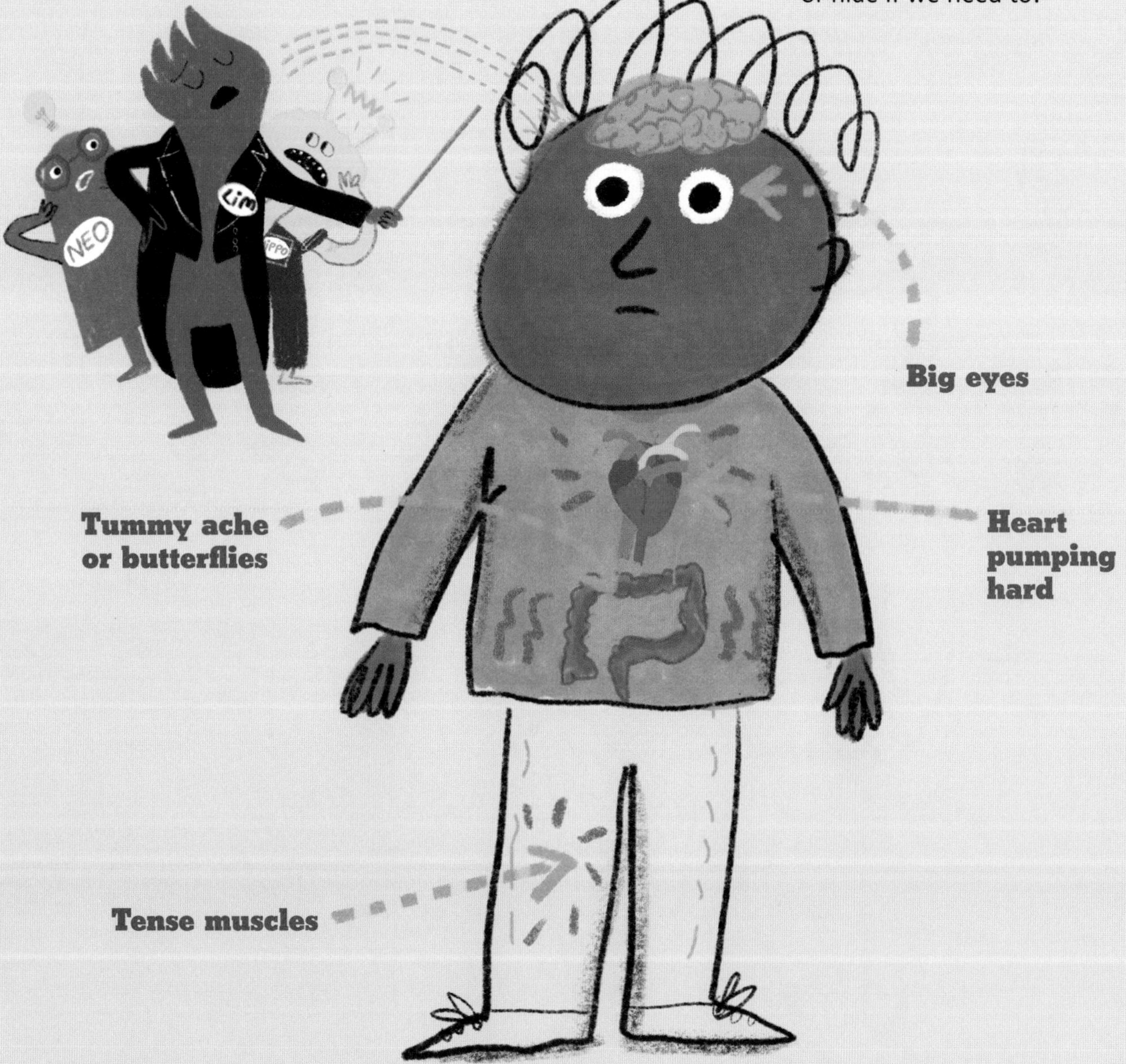

Big eyes

**Tummy ache
or butterflies**

**Heart
pumping
hard**

Tense muscles

Why does my tummy feel funny?

Have you ever noticed that when you feel worried, your tummy feels funny? It might feel like you have butterflies fluttering around inside, or maybe it feels a bit like a tummy ache.

When **Lim** sends messengers to make our heart pump harder, those messengers also move energy to the places they think we need it most.

They take energy **away** from our tummies digesting our food and move it to our **big muscles.** This can make our tummies feel a little icky or weird.

Worry Keeps Us Safe

Humans have been around for a very long time, and worry has helped us survive. But for people living today, most of the time we do not need to run or fight or hide from what makes us worried.

If you are feeling very worried or scared about something, it's always a good idea to talk to a grown-up you trust.

What makes you worried?

Just like with all the other emotions, worry is something everyone feels sometimes. I wonder what kinds of things you worry about?

SPARKLY SETTLING POTION

Make an EMOTION POTION!

Sometimes our worries pile up and they are all we can think about. This emotion potion helps slow our thoughts so we can calm down a little and take a break from all that worrying.

YOU'LL NEED

- 1 cup hot water
- ¼ cup glitter glue (regular or glow-in-the-dark)
- A small bowl
- A whisk
- Fine glitter
- Food coloring that matches your glitter
- A funnel
- An empty plastic bottle like a small water bottle
- Superglue

1 Pour the hot water and glitter glue into the bowl and whisk them together.

2 Add glitter, a little at a time as needed, to make your potion very sparkly.

3 Add one drop of food coloring at a time, mixing well, until you get the color you want.

TRY OUT YOUR SETTLING POTION

Give your settling potion a good shake. Now, slowly breathe in and out
while you watch the glitter settle. If you start to think of worries,
help **Neo** by focusing on the glitter and slowing your breathing down.

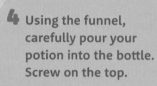

How do you
feel when you
watch the glitter
SLOWLY FALLING
through the
bottle?

4 Using the funnel,
carefully pour your
potion into the bottle.
Screw on the top.

5 Give your potion a good
shake and then watch
it settle. If you want it
to settle more quickly,
add more hot water.
If you want it to settle
more slowly, add more
glitter glue.

6 Once you are happy with
how your glitter
settles, use superglue
to secure the top.
No one wants a gluey
glittery mess all over!

Can you
feel your
HEARTBEAT
slowing down?

Do you ever feel shy?

Sometimes our worries make us want to hide. Have you ever felt worried around new people? We usually call that feeling *shy*, but shyness is a type of worry!

Sometimes we feel so **nervous** and shy that we don't want to do something we had really looked forward to.

Has your **shyness** ever kept you from doing something you were excited about?

Did you know that **nervous** and **excited** feelings come from the very same messengers in your body? They are both a mixture of adrenaline and cortisol.

Be a worry warrior!

Neo's most important job is to help us think. When we feel nervous, Neo is telling us a story that something bad is going to happen. Remember, everyone feels worried sometimes. But you can be a Worry Warrior and help Neo tell a new story.

Neo's Nervous Story sounds something like this:

A Worry Warrior tells a new story:

I can't!
I'm too scared!

My brain friends are giving me a gift of energy!
My body is excited and ready to go!

Can you think of a time when you were nervous about doing something?

How could you be a **Worry Warrior** and help Neo tell a new story so that next time you'll be ready to go?

over-whelmed

Have you ever noticed that sometimes you have more than one feeling at a time and your emotions feel all mixed up? It can feel like a giant wave of emotion rushing around and crashing inside of you! What's going on?!

We can feel overwhelmed when we are feeling lots of emotions all at once. We can also feel over-whelmed when one feeling seems to grow really BIG.

What's happening in my body when I feel overwhelmed?

When we have crazy mixed-up feelings, we can feel overwhelmed. This happens when **Amy** starts sending a lot of signals all at once. **Hippo** and **Neo** don't seem to know how to help, and **Lim** starts sending different messengers all over the place. It's like a tidal wave of messengers!

Have you ever felt overwhelmed?

Were you crying a lot, or having a hard time breathing?

Was it hard to feel comforted?

Did you feel very tired afterward?

Lots of mixed-up messengers!

Trouble breathing

Tears won't stop

MIXED-UP POTION

Make an EMOTION POTION!

Sometimes it feels like lots of mixed-up emotions are bubbling around inside. This can definitely be overwhelming!

Try making this Mixed-Up Potion that starts off bubbly and swirly. Then watch as it slowly settles.

YOU'LL NEED

An empty plastic bottle like a 16-ounce water bottle

Hot tap water

Food coloring

Vegetable oil or baby oil (enough to nearly fill your bottle)

1 Alka-Seltzer tablet

1 Fill the bottle about one-quarter of the way with hot tap water (the hotter the water, the faster the bubbles).

2 Add about 5 drops of food coloring to the water.

3 Fill the bottle the rest of the way with oil, leaving a little space at the top.

4 Break the Alka-Seltzer tablet into a few pieces and drop them into the bottle one at a time.

5 Watch your potion swirl and the bubbles rise and fall!

TIP!
Put the top on your Mixed-Up Potion and keep it somewhere safe. You can use it again just by dropping in another Alka-Seltzer tablet!

How long does it take for your potion to **CALM** and settle again?

Can you think of a time when you felt overwhelmed with mixed-up emotions? What made you feel better?

Swirly paper for calm coloring

When we feel the wave of overwhelm coming, it can really help to do a calm activity like coloring. Try making this special swirly paper that you can color on the next time you feel overwhelmed.

YOU'LL NEED

A rubber spatula

Shaving foam

A large sheet tray

Food coloring

A pencil

Sturdy paper

A ruler

You can color in the swirls, or use a dark marker to doodle on top of them.

1 Using the spatula, spread shaving foam over the tray. Cover a space as big as your paper.

2 Drip food coloring all over the foam. Use lots of colors!

3 Take your pencil and make swirly patterns in the foam.

4 Lay your paper over the foam and gently pat all over.

5 Carefully peel the paper off the foam. Use the ruler to scrape the foam off the paper to reveal your swirly pattern! Let the paper dry.

Tell a Story About How You Feel

Have you ever noticed that talking about your emotions helps you feel better? That's because you are helping **Neo** tell **Lim** a story. Do you ever feel better when someone reads you a story? You're just like **Lim**!

Let's help **Neo** tell a story. When **Neo** tells **Lim** this story, it works like magic, and **Lim** feels better. When **Lim** feels better, she stops sending the tidal wave of messengers, and then we don't feel overwhelmed.

Remember, Neo's job is to help us THINK.

To practice telling this story, get a piece of paper and set it up like this:

If you need help writing, ask a grown-up. Now think of any emotion and put that emotion in the blank next to "I feel."

Then think about a time when you have felt that emotion. Write about that time in the blank after "About."

Finally, think about why you felt that way, and write it after "Because."

When you're finished, say the whole story out loud. **How do you feel?**

I feel _____

About _____

Because _____

Now that you've practiced, you are ready to help **Neo** tell **Lim** a story the next time you feel overwhelmed!

Goodbye,
friends!
See you soon!

Dear Grown-Ups,

Have you ever noticed that feelings can be really complicated and overwhelming and sometimes feel like they come right out of the blue? Most of us have thought to ourselves, "Why on earth am I feeling like this right now?" Or "Why did I just do that?!" When our own emotional states feel like a mystery at times, how are we supposed to help our kids navigate theirs?

If we are lucky, we know a couple of feelings words and can label our feelings pretty accurately. And if we're really lucky, we've picked up some healthy coping skills along the way. But most of us don't know the physiology and neuroscience behind what makes us feel and do things, so we don't know what kinds of coping skills work with which kinds of feelings, and certainly not WHY those things work!

Even as loving and caring grown-ups who want to help our kids thrive, sometimes helping them learn to cope seems insurmountable. As soon as our kids have mastered one emotional upheaval, the next meltdown is around the corner. Maybe the next two if they are hungry or tired!

Consider this book your (and your child's) guide to navigating the emotional landscape that exists within our bodies. Our brains and nervous systems are incredibly complex, but this book breaks down the basics so your child can have a deeper ability to reflect, to cope, to enhance their own resilience, and to grow closer with you while becoming more self-sufficient.

I encourage you to read through this book on your own, and then share it with your child.

Thank you for reading!
JEN DAILY, LICSW

Materials List for Activities and Potions

from the kitchen or bathroom:

- Baking soda
- Bowls (medium and small)
- Clear vase or large jar
- Contact lens solution
- Cornstarch
- Cotton balls
- Eyedropper
- Food coloring
- Funnel
- Jar or cup
- Shaving foam
- Sheet tray
- Spatula
- Vinegar
- Whisk

from the craft closet:

- Fine glitter
- Glitter glue
- Paper (sturdy, smooth drawing paper)
- Plastic bottles (choose ones that feels good in your hand!)
- Ruler
- Straw
- Superglue
- White school glue

For Amelia, for Luna, and for C, thank you for inspiring *The Magical Science of Feelings.*
And to all the families who have trusted me along the way, thank you.

The mission of Storey Publishing is to serve our customers by publishing practical information that encourages personal independence in harmony with the environment.

EDITED BY Hannah Fries
ART DIRECTION AND BOOK DESIGN BY Carolyn Eckert
TEXT PRODUCTION BY Jennifer Jepson Smith
ILLUSTRATIONS BY © 2024 Gwen Millward

Storey Publishing
210 MASS MoCA Way
North Adams, MA 01247
storey.com

Storey Publishing is an imprint of Workman Publishing, a division of Hachette Book Group, Inc., 1290 Avenue of the Americas, New York, NY 10104. The Storey Publishing name and logo are registered trademarks of Hachette Book Group, Inc.

Distributed in Europe by Hachette Livre, 58 rue Jean Bleuzen, 92 178 Vanves Cedex, France

Distributed in the United Kingdom by Hachette Book Group, UK, Carmelite House, 50 Victoria Embankment, London EC4Y 0DZ

ISBNs: 978-1-63586-754-1: (paper over board); 978-1-63586-755-8 (ebook)

Printed in China by R. R. Donnelley on paper from responsible sources
RRD-S
10 9 8 7 6 5 4 3 2 1

Library of Congress Cataloging-in-Publication Data on file